Mr. Wilson Is Our Crossing Guard

Declan Parnell

Rosen REAL READERS

I0809771

Rosen Classroom™
New York

Mr. Wilson works at
our school.

He is our crossing guard.

He holds a stop sign.

He tells cars to stop.

He helps us cross the street.

He keeps us safe.

Words To Know

crossing guard

school

stop sign